LIKE WATER

Ivory Bennett

BookLeaf Publishing
India | USA | UK

Like Water © 2021 Ivory Bennett

Presentation by *BookLeaf Publishing*

Web: www.bookleafpub.com

E-mail: info@bookleafpub.com

ISBN: 9789358738728

First Edition 2021

Here's to becoming our ancestors' wildest dreams…

TABLE OF CONTENTS

1. DEAR DACA

An old man once told me about the American dream.
He was barefoot and shucking white corn.
His back was bent from years of hard work,
and his fingers read of routine and war.
He told me about borders and bridges,
cultures crossing over one another.
He told me about jungles and judges –
the only difference between the two was one was of God and
one wasn't.
He told me about loss and of love,
and planting seeds that you may never see grow.
He told me about investments in self,
and investments in what will come long after you're gone.
He told me to search for my purpose with my fingers and
with my heart.
"The first step," he said, "is to be courageous and just. That is
the only way to start."
This man, he shared with me a dream deferred, as he looked
me in my eyes.
He told me, "Take action, dear child, and arrive at these
things you have heard.

2. WORTHY

Even small things
can be bold,
beautiful, and loud.

Much like the
stillness of silence
after chaos.

3. I CRIED.

I cried.
And a mist fell
that covered the
greenness
of the grass,
the white and blue
of the sky.

You cried.
And a monsoon
rushed into the
valley of your pain.
Breaking bridges,
uplifting trees,
seeping deep into
the earth to drown
all things rooted.

Even the sun
could not dry
your tears.

4. WHEN WOMEN PREY

There are women whose
breasts have been
weaponized
against children.

Whose hands hurt
more than they heal.
Whose fingers land
like daggers on
unsuspecting innocents.

Whose lips carve craters
wherever they land.
Whose words cast spells
of insidious suffering.

Whose wombs are
wrought with encrypted
etchings of the
grieving ghouls,
lured there by the
pretenses of promise.

When women prey,
they baptize their pillaged
in carnal, crimson-
clad canals.

It always takes me aback.

5. I USED TO FEEL FOR THEM

in the tips of her fingers.
The way they arched,
and hung low
reminded me of weeping willows
swaying in the breeze-
carrying the scent of summer
sweet berries and cool mint.
Soft as the pillowy centers of small flowers that lay gayly in
adoration of the sun.

I used to hear them
in the bellow of her laughter.
Sweetened with time.
Sometimes, muddled with the memories of past pleasures.
But, always willing to share.
Happiness and joy,
heirlooms gifted through smiles and
kisses planted on one's forehead.

I used to smell them
at the nape of her neck.
Just above her bosom
- full of love that poured into me
with every heartfelt hug.
Warm with worth -
pricelessness -
feelings of forever.

Now, I seek these things in self.

The strength of those before me.
Their solace adorns the corridors of my soul,
And I gently knock on each door,
singing softly to myself the spirituals
that fueled my ancestors -
Even in the most bleak, shadow-filled times.
Gathering answers,
in my wicker basket
loomed of their wisdom,
collecting deep in my spirit,
reminders of what once was and
encouragement for what will be.

6. THE ARTIST

Look.
I still bear the marks he
molded into my skin.
Crafted melanin.
I am his statue.

He says the crack he placed
over my lip
was his special touch -
to remind me that he owns
my laughter. My voice.
Any song I've sung, he orchestrated.

He tells me,
while he wraps his thumb and fingers around my neck
to direct the ebb and
flow of my breath,
that he owns that, too. My wind.

He's given me great poetry.
And I've given him
bone and flesh.
Blood and beat.
Breath and body.

7. MOTHER WOUND

I don't know what to do with the sadness I feel for my mother. When the words she says aren't hurtful. When the somberness of her voice tells my heart she understands the pain she's caused us. When the helplessness of her body jumps into my fingertips, like the aftershock of an earthquake.

I don't know what to do with the sadness I feel for my mother. The tears, they have permission to break. Their rivers are steady and full with an unexpectedly strong undercurrent, that threatens to drown me daily. Not just my tears. But, tears of my mother's mother. Tears of my sisters. And uncles. Tears of my mother's lovers - unable to quite understand the loss of someone who is still here. Grief is heavy. And fast. And wet. And strong. Sometimes, unmoving. Always available to someone, somewhere, concerning something.

I don't know what to do with the sadness I feel for my mother. It's not something I want to re-gift. I desire to not re-package that pain and force it on others, or even myself. That's unfair. She doesn't want that. Neither do I.

I don't know what to do with the sadness I feel for my mother. I can't keep it inside of me - it's the kind of thing that grows exponentially. It's the kind of tenacious vine that attaches to all parts, even with no water or sunshine. It's the kind of thing that leaves an imprint, threatening to return, even after being ripped from its roots.

8.   30 MOONS

Between her legs
are revolutions:
one routed womb
writhes revelations,
rugged roots, and
rebel nations.

9. INCENSED

Her anger slithers
like water drops
down a foggy pane.
Or, like sweat beads
clinging to hot skin.
I hear past the rage,
a soft whisper of pain.

He sits in silence.
Alone, he finds himself.
Wading in pools of pain
that run red - full of fury.
Its vapors burning the pools of his
moon-shaped eyes.
Salt dries on the
bridge of his nose
as he finds his breath.

10. MEMORY

For me, memory is geographic.
I see pain in the hills.
And joy in the valleys.
Rivers flow of my tears.
Paths remind me of years.

Here, under this tree lies laughter.
Under this bridge, surprise.
Fear rest on that cliff, yonder.
The future floats along those tree lines.

11. GOOD MOURNING

When anger approaches me,
callously clothed in unkindness,
igniting relentless infernos
torched with wicked words
carving lit paths of
cruel-crusted coals,
so that none may pass
its fear-fortified fences
I greet the grieving,
who suffer in silent
stanzas of painful poetry.

12. PAPER CRANE KISSES

I prefer to whisper
under the moonlight.
Our love isn't loud,
it is resounding,
unapologetically, so.

It makes me wonder
where you've been
all this time.
Searching for one another
in the voids of others.
Only I can fill you.

And I often forgot,
the hurt I
invited in
listening to love
cradled in chaos
and misfortune.

13. UNEXPECTED INSECURITIES

Unexpected insecurities
arise during times of uncertainty.
And I'm curious, you see,
to know the invader
who lives in me.

I greet her and extend her
a place in my journey,
a seat at my table.
She teaches me with her secrets.
I thank her as she leaves.

14. UNATTRACTIVE

You are unshapely.
You smell unpleasant,
of mistrust and deceit.
You fear you.
So, I walk away without turning my back,
Tracking your eyes until my nearest exit.

You are unkind.
You hurl your power
in whirlwinds of confusion
set during the most inept times.
Like, a child,
whining for the attention of a mother
who just plucked it from one empty nipple,
to place it on the other. Full. Just for you.

Full of hurt,
you resist healing.
And assign strength to your emptiness.
You. Are not. Available.
To me. Or, yourself.
Anyone, really.
Little do you know.

You are fickle.
Often fumbling for understanding.
Cloaked in absurd assurance.
Only fooling those like you.
I see past that.

15. THE POINT OF IT ALL

Tell your stories.
Sing your songs.
Ask for forgiveness,
Humbly right your wrongs.
Walk in compassion.
Seek to understand.
Give thanks for the journey.
And always lend a helping hand.

But, a hurting heart
Doesn't exist just for making great art.
Don't sing your sadness,
As a means to entertain.
You deserve attention that isn't detrimental
Or derogatory to your name.

16. DEAR HUSBAND:

I've written you
all over my body.
And I still have space
to write more.
So that when I walk,
I leave behind
imprints of both
you and me.

17. SOBRIETY

Not all drugs are
foreign objects that
enter the body.

Some intoxicants
originate from within
the mind or the heart.

Feelings:
imagery evoked in
emotions that can create a
drunkard of the mind.

18. GPS

The rise and fall of your chest
is the beginning and the
end of my horizon.
I look to your arteries for direction,
a genetic map to my footpath.
My purpose ebbs and
flows from the magnificent
omnipotence of your heart -
beating effortlessly, yet earnestly.
I live for you.

19.SHE CRYIN'

Why she cryin'?
Don't she know
we all feel pain?
Been gutted wit' the
same sharp blade?

Why she cryin'?
Who she think she is?

Tell 'ah to close
up my door.
I don't let out that pain -
I done paid too much to
keep it thata way.

Why she cryin'?
Who she think she is?

Tell 'ah go walk in dat rain.
Ain't too much
ta lose or gain.
Don't go pushin'
'gainst dat ol' grain.

20. UNINTERRUPTED JOY

It is my daily prayer that children
whose laughter falls like flower petals
floating in a summery breeze,
whose eyes read in sparkles of continuous curiosity,
whose hearts beat faithfully like the burning core of the
earth's inward drum,
whose hands crawl and creep fearlessly among the unknown,
whose flesh repairs itself anew in strength that feels soft to
the touch,
whose ears make music of mundane mutterings,
whose feet find footing on the most imperceptible paths,
whose minds are limitless with imagination unparalleled only
by God, Herself,
whose hearts have endless capacities to love,
whose perceptions remain unmuddled by callous judgment,
never know the disjointed existence
of unnecessary suffering.

Brown girl.
Why does our
hair defy gravity?
Absorbing water, it blossoms
into fields of curling flowers
whose petals reach earnestly
towards the skies
in worship of God's sun?
A God whom we meet
with oils, baptizing every
strand in intentional adoration.
Tired, we toil and we tease.
And we grow -
because we carry
the sky on our heads.

22. SISTERS

Together,
we pierced raindrops
in an attempt to weave
them into a necklace
that we might wear,
in lieu of our tears.

23. REVERENTLY REMEMBER ME

In reverence,
I want to remember your sweetness.

I want to hear music in the way
that you call my name.
Your touch, is an honor and privilege -
may the warmth of recollections
remain even after the last grazing of your fingertips.
Your smile, a lamp in an ocean of darkness.
The depths of your joy shines radiantly,
reflecting the best parts of me I never knew
or saw.

In reverence,
I want to remember your softness.

The gentleness in your guidance -
a persistent patience, unwavering and foundational.
Your laugh, an ancestrally orchestrated
gathering of goodness.
A welcome rapturing of all things kind,
intentional hopefulness.

In reverence,
I want to remember.

24. CONDITIONS

"If I love you,
I cannot lie to you."
Which is why I move
in ways that may seem cautious.
You see the entire me,
without limitations -
an intentional act of vulnerability
that only you evoke.

If I love you,
I cannot give you
mere pieces of me.
I offer the enormity of my soul,
a spirit rooted in this body and
bone and blood and flesh
is submitted at the altar of
your existence, always
in all ways.

I want to touch you.
But, not in the way you'd imagine.
I wonder, where are your soft places?
How many hearts have you broken?
And, do you even care?

You're so hard.
Yet, penetrable.
And it's funny...
Because men seem to think they are the only ones to enter
into someone so deeply.

What makes you cry?
And how do you feel about it?
Is it something you hide from others?
Have you ever bathed in sadness?
Do you run to women to wash away the pain for you?

You wonder, I'm sure,
What I think of you.
You have just as many,
If not more
Insecurities than women.
Men just wear them differently.
It's kind of like the saying,
"It's not what you wear,
It's how you wear it.
Or, if it wears you."

What wears you?
What fantasies keep you up at night?

Do you actually have desires?
Do you actually want love?
Or, do you want control?
Power.
Do you want someone
who will reflect such carnal desires?
Or, someone who will balance out the darkness within you
with her light?

I wish you could just be
honest with your wants
And needs
And intentions.
It could all be so simple.

26. IMMIGRATION

My great grandmother was known to make mountains of
mole hills.
Out in the desert, she would say, is where the possibilities are
endless.
When the sun set, the moon gave way to a new place, a new
time –
time was measured in sunsets and moons.
She knew every constellation.

In the city, I saw her eyes fill with winter.
Cold, she would always be searching for the sun and the
moon above the towering buildings. She missed her friends in
the sky and would reach for them in the night with her
fingertips.

She would tell me, "When I die, take me home. Take me back
to my country and spread me across the land."

27. MILK + MUSES

Must I suckle you from
the nipple of my breast,
in order for you to feel
from the inside out
the radiant warmth of the
love I have for you?

28. GRIEF

Heartache feels like
cradling a stillborn
who was once wrapped up in womb,
then thrust into your arms
before the tears have
dried up from the wells of your eyes.
The wounded womb
and the wounded heart
have more in common than one might think - they both
mourn death and wield life.

29. ENTRÉE

Many people have taken my sadness home,
in a stained brown-paper bag.

Made it a side dish in their meals.
Dipped it away, at the end of day.

Talked about it when they didn't
want to talk about it, still.

I'm sure they still carry its
taste in their hearts.
And it bubbles up occasionally,
like an indigestion of the soul.

The truth,
it does not lie.
It is always standing
on solid ground.